Just a Bend

Just a Bend

Ekpe Inyang

Illustrated by
Marie-Brenda Offy Inyang

Spears Books
Denver, Colorado

Spears Books
An Imprint of Spears Media Press LLC
7830 W. Alameda Ave, Suite 103-247
Denver, CO 80226
United States of America

First Published in the United States of America in 2020 by Spears Books
www.spearsmedia.com
info@spearsmedia.com
Information on this title: www.spearsmedia.com/just-a-bend

ISBN: 9781942876595 (Paperback)
Also available in Kindle

Cover design by Doh Kambem
Text design and typesetting by Spears Media Press LLC, Denver, CO

For my late parents, Helen Offiong and Anthony Inyang,
late wife, Eni Inyang and
my children, Okum, Arah, Beya, Offy, and Joy

Contents

FOREWORD

Nature, destruction, and an urgent call for action! *Just a Bend*, a rich collection of poems, sounds a loud call to save Mother Earth and humanity from wanton destruction.

This collection highlights the vision of Ekpe Inyang as he recollects many situations, which reflects his rich experience from childhood to adulthood. As a child, his first contact was with nature – the biophysical in its pure state. He recaptures the splendour of nature; he is appalled by its wanton destruction. As an adult, he gives a first-hand glimpse of human nature and takes a cursory look at our Mother Earth whilst proposing solutions to the many man-made problems.

An outstanding educator, Ekpe Inyang focuses on the immediate issues through lines that remain, as it were, in our mouth; due to the beauty, we chew the words and capture the meaning and ultimately, take action! That's the goal of his poetry; appeal for a change in attitude that leads to action to resolve the problems that plague our earth and us!

The title is very apt - *Just a Bend*. The path we have been trudging on is crooked! But we should not despair! Ekpe Inyang insists that we should take a bend and veer off this crooked path onto a new one! To do so, a change of attitude and a strong yearning for action are needed.

Ekpe has used his rich experience to produce a scintillating piece that takes us through a breath-taking poetic journey, exposing us to various types of poems that address myriad issues that confront us today.

— Daniel Agoons, *Literary Critic*

In life, there are starters and there are finishers. But to finish properly it's important to know how it's started.

Similarly, in life, there are producers and there are consumers. But to consume sustainably, it might be a good idea to, at least, know what it takes to produce.

Also, in life, there are creators and there are critics. The two need to understand and accept each other well to help them refine the guides that support their endeavours.

Again, in life, there are friends and there are foes. The two also need to understand each other well to help them redefine their purposes.

Yet again, in life, there are winners and there are losers. It's critically important for the two to understand the strategies and purposes of each other - and in various circumstances - to better appreciate the essence of winning or losing.

Ekpe Inyang, 4 August 2019

Just
a
Bend

No room for excuses.
No time for regrets.
Only moments for celebration.
Even in the most stressful and unproductive environment,
you can still find a reason and create some space to be
productive.

- Ekpe Inyang, 2019

Put Down the Barrels

(A song For Mother Africa)

Ladies and gentlemen
    Join me to make this song
        For Mother Africa
            Torn by long, long wars

Let's call for love and peace
    Devoid of such deceit
        Promoting endless wars
            That make us mourn daily

Weld a better Africa
    Ensure lasting peace
        You give the chorus
        I'll take the verses

Put down the barrels
    Pick up the long mikes
        Let's move to table
            And sit for dialogue

Go park the war trucks
    Climb on the train
        Lay down the weapons
            Let's vote for peace

Put down the barrels
    Pick up the long mikes
        Let's move to table
            And talk for peace

Babies are crying
    Mothers are dying

The heat is rising
Thousands are dying

Put down the barrels
Pick up the long mikes
Let's move to table
And sit for dialogue

Why do you build now
Only to destroy soon?
Your houses burnt down
Your streets deserted

Put down the barrels
Pick up the long mikes
Let's move to table
And talk for peace

Men hide in bushes
Women bear bruises
Children keep rushes
Hiding in churches

Put down the barrels
Pick up the long mikes
Let's move to table
And sit for dialogue

What are you doing
To Mother Africa?
She is so shrunken
Look at her jaws

Put down the barrels
Pick up the long mikes
Let's move to table
And talk for peace

17 April 2018

Give Him His Right

Turn thou on soon the wise green light
With only the red it's been tight
Bent on displaying your great might?
To stop thou now the endless fight
Contemplate giving him his right

9 March 2018

Hiding the Act

It happens almost everywhere
Yet it is like it happens not at all
As silence often greets such acts
When salaries so swell to hide
Nefarious acts that decimate

15 March 2018

Changing Climes

      The sky is choking
With incessant smoke from chimneys
Forests are
      Vanishing in lightning speed
Temperatures
Rising yearly
      Climes
Changing
Winds growing wild
      Roofs
Lifted off daily
Crops failing
      Hunger rising
Incomes
Plummeting
      Vulnerable communities
Rendered far more vulnerable
Death toll
      Soaring high

18 May 2018

Poetico-Dramatic Nonsense

(On my birthday)

No prying
No crying
Keep trying

Keep typing

More frying
More drying
Keep tying

Keep typing

No flying
No dying
Keep buying

Keep typing

More hiding
More hiking
Keep mining

Keep typing

15 September 2018

Hong Kong

"Hong Kong confirmed beautiful!!! Hello, where do I...?" "No, hahaha, no."
"OK, here. In Chinese. My hotel. Need a taxi" "Yes. Straight."
Now I had learnt communication's more of emotions behind words, as
I met.
Great people with body language radiating positive energy, welcoming,

Knowing, perhaps, that not speaking or reading Chinese doesn't mean
One is stupid; hence most I met tried hard to communicate,
No matter how little we understood each other. What a
Great experience communicating largely with little or no spoken language!

24 September 2018

On Memories Lost

Been sailing through the sky
Of centuries past
All along with eye
On memories lost
Now see clear paintings of primal blast
That blew gases into the living ball of dust
Now being blasted...degraded towards void last

18 September 2018

New Delhi

Never stop striving
Ever for the best
With just a few more

Doses of effort we can make the
Earth a really wonderful place and
Life will be full of love and care
Hospitality a strong currency
India more than simply incredible

27 January 2019

Or, Rather, Invitingly Deceitful?

I peeped through
My gaping hotel window
And saw the large yellow ball
Like flowers that still dress the trees
Rising from the horizon
Then I know what to put on
I thought - my light yellow outfit
But I stepped out to catch our bus
And got a bite of freezing air and yelled
You've been deceitfully inviting
Or, rather, invitingly deceitful?

29 January 2019

My Prayer

(especially for the youth & the old all over the world)

Let my labour
Turn to favour

Disappointment
To appointment

Near demotion
To promotion

Demolition
Consecration

Air pollution
Sure ablution

Home frustration
Famed migration

From dark background
To bright foreground

Clear confusion
To great vision

From poverty
To property

From being zero
To sweet hero

17 February 2019

Happy Valentine's Day

How much of me you do really cherish
And how of you I do really love can be
Proven by how much we share in common
Providing mutual care and support in times
Yet to find us back in our comfort zones

Veiled love and care can perish unnoticed
And just to prove you really care show overt
Love by sending this message to everyone
Enclosed in your clear heart of genuine love
Never for a day under consideration of substitution
Totally glued to your frame of genuine love though
Initially there were moments of misunderstandings; but
Now that you have reached this level of comprehension
Every effort should be made never to drop to lower rungs
Do it and do it and do it again and again and again and again
And you will see the glorious brightness of success in your life
Yes, you can; send this piece of peace to all your loved ones

12 February 2019

Beware 23rd!

Korob, Kiong, efen a Kitork
I salute you all in sincerity
And love...but with fear in my heart

Don't forget we children of Kitork
Can be counted on fingers
And every head named
Without consulting a register

We are undoubtedly the most endangered
Set on planet Earth - minority of minorities
Yet I see some of us ready to face live bullets

Children of Kitork have never been this
Manipulated by politics that has paid us not
Except for the few whom we serve but who soon
Forget we ever risked our lives for their protection

Kitork children of distant past fought battles
Not to swell the stomachs of their masters
But for our land to extend and selves to defend

Don't forget our numerical disadvantage
Which we should fight to strengthen and not plunge
Ourselves into acts that instead will weaken
As I see some of us madly pitted against each other

What for? We have been in this for so long
Risking our lives, elevating our masters
Each camp twisting the cards and counts
Yet see our roads and other public amenities
Children of Kitork, today I call upon you:
Pick up the wisdom of Obon Soromon
And drop the myopia of Kitukitu. Beware 23rd!
19 February 2019

Nature

When storms grow wild
And tree boughs break
Leaves flying left and right
Dust forming thick haze
Then bullet-like drops
Hit roofs so hard
You'll hardly hear
Any sound around
Save the mad aerial war
And your bounding heart
Nature can sometimes
Be so terrifying, like illness
To keep men as humble
As when they were born

20 February 2019

The plant

Birds and insects
Pay regular homage
To her for the flowers
That house sugary wells

Browsers always
There for the leaves
Monkeys transmuting
Via interlocking boughs

Feasting mostly on fruits
Some falling on forest floor
For ungulates that may
Also go for bark of stem

Anchored by roots growing
Deep into soil away from
Predation, avoiding instant
Withering of the plant

20 February 2019

When I'm Alive

Don't give me food
Only when I'm sick
Give it to me when
I have the appetite
To prevent the illness

Don't talk against me
When I've shown my back
Talk against me when
I'm around to defend or
Explain what you don't know

Don't celebrate me
When I'm dead
Celebrate me when I live
To see how much
I'm valued and appreciated

21 February 2019

New Horizons

(In honour of a Cameroonian Conservation Guru)

Handsome and handy Hanson
Always with a reassuring smile, but
Never failing to make cautionary
Statements when it comes to adhering to the
Organization's code of conduct
Never allowing feet to take wrong tracks

Njiforti is the name, the Nji, Prince, but
Just reflect and decide if here he is only the son of a Prince
In conservation, undoubtedly, he is King
From the 80's he's seen landscapes rolling and heard lions roaring
Organizationally and ecologically, even culturally; all this
Resonating the vision and passion he bears intimately as
Torchlight to lead colleagues to new horizons
In conservation for Culture-Nature harmony assurance

26 February 2019

Germund Sellgren

(for a colleague, an ESD pundit and a brother-in-deed)

Great mind that cannot be seen from its simplicity
Ever positive, proactive and ready to inspire others
Rooted in a culture of mutual respect, love and care
Memories that will never die amongst the ESD family
United by a vision of creating a sustainable future
Nourishing youth with ideas on green entrepreneurship
Demonstrating innovations never before imagined

Sorry, we shall miss a professional from the scene...but
Encouraged we should be as he is very much around
Love will always push him to extend his hand to hold up the
Light that must never die but shine to show the way to
Gain the much needed sustainable development by
Revisiting and revamping the fast waning sustainability path to
Ensure, unwaveringly, that pedagogy applied guarantees that
Nature inspires Culture to develop cities of great harmony

19 March 2018

Weird

Come, come, come
Help me confirm
What I've been seeing

Rivers flowing uphill?
Rain falling skyward?
Rocks falling from the sky?

Tree roots growing towards the sun?
Leaves growing into the soil?
Blood oozing from the earth?

Dogs feasting on grass?
Goats devouring hyenas?
Humans changing skins like snakes?

It wasn't just yesterday
I started observing
These weird events

Seven long seasons
Have been my period of torment
Observing these sinister scenes

But I had kept it close to my chest
And all along I've been thinking
My eyes were failing

I've always thought telling this
Would earn me the name I hate to hear
But just a moment ago my grandchild

Confirmed what I've been seeing
Year after year after year after year

But I thought he was daydreaming

A dog had come barking so wildly
As it espied the hideous replay but
I concluded it was seeing its shadow

Now I need an adult like you
An adult with honesty and dignity
To come confirm what I see

26 April 2019

No Peace at All

Killings and kidnappings
Burnings and beheadings
Intimidations and incriminations
Cruelty at its peak by civil crooks
Boiling waters of war boreholes

28 April 2019

Cry of a Tired Granddaddy

It all started many seasons ago when
I was still on the generosity of breast milk
Two pieces of land were blindly merged
Instead of drifted by culture tectonics

It wasn't quite a forced marriage though
Or so it is generally acknowledged but
It's certainly one flawed by selfishness
And lack of concrete choices to make

Now it's clear it's been one of long
Bitter period of convenience in which
One half of the heart now erupts from
Long seasons of unending oppression

Now granddaddy, larvae flows steadily
And I'm on frequent house-arrest for
Being borne into two pieces forged into
One and indivisible piece without peace

30 April, 2019

Happy Labour Day

Have a silent moment to reflect
Adding meaningful words of
Prayer for good health, peace and
Prosperity assured by equality
Yes, you have

Laboured for a year now
And need not only national recognition
But blessings from God who is
On high and who
Until now has been your strength and
Rock on which you stand and

Daily build your plans towards
Ameliorating
Your livelihood and state of the world

1 May 2019

The Crab

The crab
What a structure
Looks so frightful

The crab
Showing off its pincers
Veike a scorpion

The crab
See the way it stands
like a tortoise

The crab
See its movements
So, so crafty

The crab
Just the way it feeds
Seems so sly and selfish

The crab
In armour of calcium
Ready for mum's pot

4 May 2019

Ruth Fese Enie

Realistically creative but
Unrelenting in search of more impulses
Totally committed to green thought
Heart as green as the Rain

Forest that birthed and nurtured her
Enlightened in culture, a wisdom pot
Superbly
Entertaining in writing and nature

Ever smiling, thus making kids and visitors feel at home
Naturally kind and hospitable
Interested in contributing to world
Encyclopaedias of knowledge

5 May 2019

Stockholm

Saving the pride of Europe but giving it
The taste and flavour of Scandinavia
Orientating every visitor on the simple
Culture of love, peace, care and respect
Knowing we share a global village
Hospitality, equality and magnanimity
Overflowing with the green volcanic
Lava of abundance, security and safety
Measured on the scale of sustainability

Stockholm, 12 May 2019

Stay Safe

Play to stay safe
Silent in cave
Put out the bait
Catch a new date
Take us on sail
Tell a long tale

Stockholm, 11 May 2019

Strong Nerve

You have such a strong nerve
To say you still want to serve
After all the bath in red petal
That with your feet you paddle

Stockholm, 11 May 2019

Cast the Dice

Cast the dice
You'll drop the vice
Tell no lies
You killed no flies

Tell the truth
You'll marry ruth
Take a bet
You'll pet the pet

Stockholm, 11 May 2019

Measurements

Why, on earth, do you think
I am short?
Height should not be measured
With the big, bold ruler you hold
But by the level I can reach

Why do you think
You are civilized?
Civilization should not be measured
By your technological sophistication
But by its level or hue of greenness

Why do you think
We are too small?
Size should not be measured
By your observation of our bulks
But by our abilities and capabilities

Why, for God's sake, do you think
They are slow?
Slowness should not be measured
By the pace of their actions
But by what they can accomplish

Why do you think
He is blind?
Blindness should not be measured
By the physical things he can't see
But by his (in)ability to envision

Why the hell do you think
She is backward?
Backwardness should not be measured
By capitalistic indicators of growth

But on the scale of harmony with nature

Why, indeed, do you think
It is primitive?
Primitivism should not be measured
On your scale of civilization
But on that of Contribution to Nature

Measurements by us are oft subjective
Even rulers, tapes, speedometers
Barometers, thermometers...
Only give fair pictures, as there is
Nothing perfect in anything human

Stockholm, 12 May 2019

Love Without...

Love without needed emotions
Is like a skull without a brain

Love without needed emotions
Is like a head without ears

Love without needed emotions
Is like a face without eyes

Love without needed emotions
Is like a nose without nostrils

Love without needed emotions
Is like a mouth without a tongue

Stockholm, 19 May 2019

When Shall it Stop?

When shall we stop hearing
Agony-filled, heart-rending cries?
When shall we start bearing
Bloodless flag that our tears dries?

Yaounde, 21 May 2019

Peace, peace, peace

Faces, in multitudes, twisting
Stomachs, big and small, grumbling
Minds apparently perturbed
In view of daily, blunt and bold
Surreptitious interactions
Bloody transactions rife
Frightful ominous sounds
Cracking the walls of life
Painful awful sights
Seizing the last strands of hope
Villages burnt, people forced to flee
Communities drained, incapacitated.
Economic impact weighing
Steadily heavily on households
Fatherland surely not spared
Yet no sign of ceasing, really?
Must I climb that tall Iroko tree
Ascend its full height
For you to discern my agony-lazed face
As I yell, frustrated as I now feel
"Horror, horror, horror?"

Hearts silently but heavily bleed
Pounding hard on the frail walls of life
Collapsing the precarious pillars of
Miserly, meagre existence
Hearts palpitating and oscillating
In utter fear and confusion
Surely fear of the unknown
Fear of the worst that will
Surely come to pass if nothing's done
To curb the current torrent of carnage
See souls brutally wasted
Life terminated even

In its fourth month of free breath!
What offense did that baby commit?
What crime? What...?
I'm speechless!
Cruelty of the highest order
Unprecedented phenomenon
Sacrilegious acts now ubiquitous
In the noble land of my birth?
Clear demonstration of callousness
Theatre of Bestiality

I wish all this were
One big dream, a feat
A hallucination in a malaria attack
A fictional adventure novel, a fairy tale
A horror film in my wildest dreams
So I wake up suddenly one morning
Feeling so glad again on
Seeing the radiant brightness
In the light, blue sky
Enjoying the peace that once was
Yes, peace we all used to enjoy
Peace suddenly stolen from us by none
Other than the demon of all demons
Demon whose lethal force is
Bought and sprayed around fearlessly
By satanic, heartless souls
Peace, peace, peace
Peace that shall surely reign again
For all of us to freely live

En route from Yaounde to Douala, 22 May 2019

Stubborn Koko

A really stubborn Koko
Who refused to take
Their wicked koboko
Snatched their cake
Bit the nose of a Boko
Calling the villain fake

25 May 2019

Mo Kom

(Rehearsing my little Efik)

Inyang Mma
Mo kom o
Etie didie?
Efik do?
Ndito nyin
Mo do?
Ndito Okoyong
Ndito Ododop
Amanisong a Kitork
Nko mo do?
Kpukpuru mo
Edi ufan mi
Kom mo no mi o

29 May 2019

Blue Sky

Let them yell
Like big bell
Let them cry
Like dragonfly
Let us love
Like humble dove
Let's unite
And let's ignite
Making the eye
So, so bright
So, so bright
Like the blue sky

1 June 2019

Seng Dunyo

(My advice to the youth of Korob)

A kwoni mung?
Kpara a wei dobok
Kpara a babi esin
Seng dunyo

A kwoni mung?
Kpara a tara a enen
Se kwa a keme
Seng dunyo

A kwoni mung?
Kwa a tongho u se
U ka bud bien
Seng dunyo

A kwoni mung?
Buka bungo
Bu ka nyangha ibohn
Seng dunyo

Kwa eromsin engo
E beke a ngo
A se, se u nyanha
Kebern ke seng dunyo

Buka bu re
Kachang ka kebern
Ere a chom u kon ikpin
A ba seng dunyo

1 June 2019

In Search of Positive Creativity

Visit homes, hospitals; walk the streets
See challenges faced by humanity
Take a moment, look up at the sky
Admire the Sun, Moon and Stars
Walk the paths formed by those
Wondrous constellational shapes
Bathe in the full magnificence of the aura
Cast by those great celestial cities yonder
Set beyond our limited eyes and minds
Take a break and take a walk of
Nature's terrestrial and aquatic homes
In all their shapes, shades and feel
Experience the inexhaustible power
Universe has in store for us
Hike the forests, grasslands, deserts
Brave "the wilderness", "the jungle"
Face the mountains, hills & valleys
Swim the rivers, lakes and seas
Put up the sail and brave wild waters
In canoes, boats, ships, anything
That can keep us afloat and alive
Visit fascinating and enticing beaches
Walk and roll in the generous sands
White, yellow, brown and black sands
Sands that form you, them, and me
Sands above and from rocks beneath
White, yellow, brown and black
Rocks used to construct and destroy
Can you see how far we've gone?
What a great journey it has been!
Receive the energy that now flows
Into our hungry and thirsty dish
For that rare inspiration to feed
Our blood with the precious oxygen

Of positive creativity and innovation
And let it flow through our veins
To reach our pedigree, but surely, freely
Into our brains and minds and hearts
To finally find unrestrained expression
In our mouths and legs and hands
In all that is us – it's wholeness and wellness
Unlocking, unleashing our huge potentials
Buried deep in the far reaches
Of our being, deep, deep, deep
In that core of void and nothingness
In that fountain of inventiveness and ingenuity
Ready to emit in pure magnanimity
The multifarious models and strategies
Wisdom, skills, techniques, technologies
Wonders never before near the shallow well
Of our millennia's stretching imagination
To address some of the myriad daunting
Challenges faced today by humanity

2 June 2019

Have You Ever?

Have you ever heard
There is a great people called Borob
People of Korob that straddles
The nations of Cameroon and Nigeria
Subtly and peacefully uniting the two
In cross-border trade and marriages?

Have you ever made a tour of Korob
Sat on Renko, stared at Ewuri a Holmes
Gawked at Inani a Yoyo, drunk from
Akurern, climbed Inani a Batake
Awed by Esoke and consumed by
The frightful sight of Okpa a Okomo
And stories about Okpa a Fururu?

Have you ever stayed in Korob
Enjoyed the splendour of the rainforest
The immeasurable love and care
The welcoming spirit and kind hospitality
The colourful and scintillating culture
The wonderful traditional dishes:
Idio a mini-mini, ekon a irio, banana
A nduk, kakam ka nduk, bunang ba
Bukperd, urebetum, ekpang a ikwang?

Have you ever heard of the big story:
The long, long walk from far, far away
The brief stop in the grass-fields
Of Cameroon, and settlement in Kitork
Then the growth into Amakisae, Ayoyo
Ochum-Ochum, Echungane, Okoyong
Then the loss of Okoyong to Nigeria?

Have you ever heard the tales
Mothers used to tell so sorrowfully
About Okoyong once on Akarok Hill
About cries of babies of the last set
Families yet to decide to leave or not
How our great Okoyong encountered
A big river in the fullness of the rains
How a crocodile surely ferried it across
Where now it's over a hundred folds?

For years on years on years
Okoyong existed only in the tales
Schooled Korob mothers often told
To kill the laziness of hot afternoons
But reminded children of a people lost
To motivate them to go out in search
To explore Efikland where they were
Suspected to have planted their roots
And this has yielded fruits for at last
The lost has been found with great joy
Now united with brethren for progress

5 June 2019

Osere

Osere of Ekon of hills and rocks
The ancient capital of Korob culture
Who has not heard of him that wore
A skin as fair as his heart
Filled with chalk from Kitork soil?

Osere a Mburu greatest of the greats
The man who ate kolanuts grated
On a handy grater
Murmuring a song in rhythm as he did
Deep in meaning though dead of words

Osere the warm - and kind-hearted
He that made his little grater
His suit's companion wherever he went
A black suit that told vivid stories of
Huts and gongs that built ancient Kitork

Osere the unrivaled story-teller
He that blessed kids' hungry afternoons
With food stored in an old clay bowl
His share of fees from Ekwe initiates
Or those in the line to get great titles

Osere greatest teacher then on earth
Master of history learnt in great fun
Author of adventure songs and stories
Sung and told in self-same words
Renditions rendered in moving pictures

Osere the king of great Beyatang
Family that brought to Ekon Ama-erot
God of fruitfulness and shining beauty
Giver of children to those in real need

Gift a woman fetched from River Mfake

Who has not heard of Obon Osere?
Tall man whose back children fought
To scrub with a smooth Kitork stone
Enjoying his monthly stream bath
On a giant rock for body cleansing

6 June 2019

Come

Come, come, come
Women, men, and youth
Come
Come see me claim reward

Come, come, come
Friends and foes
Come
Come watch me grab award

No delay, come
Follow me, come
Friends and foes, run
Come and share in my dream

Come, ladies, come
Come, gents, come
Come, come, come
Come help me carry bags

6 June 2019

My Joy

My great Joy
Never a thing
With which to toy
Give me not a ring
I'm deep in prayer
For her great success
I call for no player
My team to buttress

7 June 2019

Health and Death

Let not your sure health
Be soon stolen by death

Stay away from things
That push one into rings

Life is so, so precious
Need to be cautious

Though you may be busy like bee
Evil soul bring yourself not to be

Near not circles of atrocities
Never live off polluting cities

Live by sharing love
Be humble like dove

7 June 2019

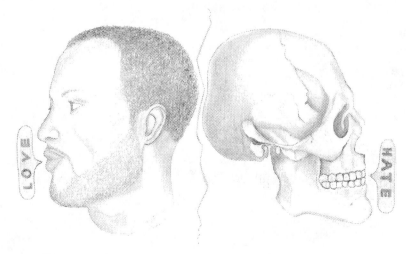

Just a Stupid Poem

Ask him questions
On poetry
Even on his simplest poems
And you'll get another difficult poem

Sit him for a chat over a drink
On drama
And you'll be transported to
The Globe Theatre

Engage him in deep conversation
On philosophy
And you'll face a wiser
Aristotle

Share with him ideas
On biology
And you'll conclude
Mendel's contribution was nothing

What about taking a walk with him
On chemistry
And you'll be angry
The periodic table is incomplete

Confront him with a problem
On mathematics and physics
And you'll discover
Einstein was no genius at all

Never ask him for advice
On astrology
Unless you want to learn how
To do an irreversible soul travel

Don't be scared, it's just a stupid poem
On absurdity
To test if you're the genius teacher
That has all the answers

7 June 2019

The New Song

I've been listening to
The drops all through the night
Even deep in my sleep
I could hear them
Chanting the new song

I've been familiar with those
Drops ever since I was born
Right from my childhood
I've heard them
Chanting the new song

On my travels to distant lands
Those drops never ceased
Defining every path and step I took
As I continued to hear them
Chanting the new song

Let's drop the old tunes
Has been the message of the drops
Drumming on our consciousness
As they continue
Chanting the new song

On our roofs, on the streets
Same message
Drumming on our consciences
As the drops continue
Chanting the new song

8 June 2019

Who Says We Can't?

Who says we can't stop
The spread of cancer,
Who says
Cancer can't be cured?

Who says we can't stop
The spread of HIV,
Who says
HIV-AIDS is incurable?

Who says we can't stop
Climate change,
Who says
Climate change is irreversible?

Who says we can't build clean
Technologies and still make huge profits,
Who says
Clean technologies are too expensive?

Who says we can't stop
The rising wars across the globe,
Who says
The wars are unstoppable?

If we can simply change the idle "can't"
To a big "can", negative thoughts to
Positive individual and collective actions,
Everything, indeed, is possible.

8 June 2019

Technologies Vs. Doxologies

With application of clean technologies
We really can make more gains
From just a few viable grains
But allow no room for undue drains
And spread of uninformed doxologies

8 June 2019

Fizzled Out Too Soon

(In memory of Prof. Anne Tanyi-Tang)

You'd been our great source
Our hope largely placed on you
As you'd been such a resource
But it fizzled out too soon

We're still contemplating
Who will really fill your place
It's not been easy ruminating
But it fizzled out too soon

There's a vacuum in the literary palace
And we continue to stretch our minds
To find one that will take your place
But it fizzled out too soon

Just at the time you're needed most
To give the palace a new face-lift
Your prowess made us start to boast
But it fizzled out too soon

Ewa's story's created such an impact
Among female youth who've read it
Each craves for success, makes a pact
But it fizzled out too soon

Life is an unpredictable journey
Ending when one least expects
Fizzles out when dripping with honey
But it fizzled out too soon

8 June 2019

Can't Get it Back Freely

You were born free
Came out freely from the womb
Cried and cried but later laughed
Crawled and walked and ran about
Played, danced and jumped freely
Learnt, unlearnt and relearnt
Challenging, improving and expanding
Your boundless faculties and territories
As you engaged in all those acts
Freely

But if today you can't
Freely do those wondrous things
Know your freedom has either been
Carelessly dropped, pawned or stolen
So freely from you at some point
And to get it back you must fight
Without hate, spears, guns and bombs
But with purpose and wits and faith in dialogue
A few wrongful keepers may turn around
And hand it back to you
Freely

9 June 2019

Fruits of Injustice

Now sleep knows not your eyelids
Your heart panics at the least rumour
Always you expect a tremor
Pondering of pits long dug to trap
Fruits of injustice

You created a bandit's empire
Turned yourself into a vampire
Sucking blood, now you know no sleep
Fruits of injustice

At the aired calling of names
Those to serve grave sentences
Your ears are always on the ground
Pricked to hear the mention of yours
Fruits of injustice

At the slightest sound of a gun
Far, far away from your precincts
You conclude the start of a revolution
Armed with bullet and bomb proofs
Fruits of injustice

Millions oft go on picnics with families
You stay glued to radio, TV and SM
Or fly away when the sky turns dark
Fruits of injustice

Counterparts stroll the streets freely
You go to toilet with a bunch of guards
You've really made yourself a prisoner
Fruits of injustice

9 June 2019

He Never Dines Alone

He never dines alone
But keeps on giving
Even to those who backbite
Throw insults or openly confront him

He never dines alone
But keeps on fighting, even
For those who backstab him, give him
Deep wounds with indelible scars

He never dines alone
But keeps on recommending
Even those who always smear his name
And run him down in front of fellow staff

He never dines alone
But keeps on supporting employment
Even from camps of overt foes
Ready to frustrate and humiliate him

He never dines alone
Knows no lines separating humans
Even those cleaning his house and office
Those recruited to serve him daily

At last there is this serious tremour
His name flagged among those
Dragged into mud, to cost him his job
But since he never dines alone

Fewer friends than foes make testimonies
In no inflated or painted statements in public
Final vindication of him; tables turn, and he
Soars to the highest rung among the staff
9 June 2019

No Him, No Poems

Without Him above
No titles for my poems
No lines, no stanzas
No better poems from me

He gives the titles
He provides all the lines
He builds the stanzas
To help me write the poems

9 June 2019

Redress

Crystal clear signs
Using pure science
Without conscience
Cannot redress
Today's express
Earth's undress

10 June 2019

Breaking Our Earth Apart

We always want to show off our great might
Prove our point to the rest of the world
Showcase military technologies, capabilities
And superior war skills, strategies and prowess
But we're, indeed, breaking our earth

We all share this one earth, our only planet
Yet with impunity we send out missiles
Millions of miles away to test and prove
We've gone this far in this new craze with
Which we're shamelessly breaking our earth

The world needs far more than military might
Something that only makes billions live in fear
Hate and plans to revenge or start fresh attacks
When a billion live below the poverty line
While we're steadily breaking our earth

We've seen all these wars in terror
And can safely say nothing really is new
Greatness must now be shown more in
Technologies hijacking wars and building peace
For we're seriously breaking our earth

Great nations should be those known with
More technologies to feed billions of mouths
To heal and bring more health to the world
Instead of pain and sorrow and soaring losses
As we're heartlessly breaking our earth

Our knowledge and skills and raw materials
To build what we now use to crack and break
We often get by cracking our earth
What a wonderful way of paying back

That we're now breaking our earth apart

10 June 2019

Wonderful Crossroads

(For my daughter, Offy, on her birthday)

Often in life many a time
You may have not a dime

You may have no idea
How from Ekon to get to Edea

Imagine that's the one place
Where you're destined to trace

And find all that you need
To succeed in life indeed

To you no dime means impossible
But think and you'll find it's possible

At crossroads pause for reflection
Never ever focus in one direction

11 June 2019

Tricks

He makes a fresh new trick
At every clock's new tick
He's always lived that way
To survive each new day
To him he's so, so wise
Yes, clever like the mice
That let go their long tails
And feed on fake sour tales
But comes that one fine day
He cannot find a ray
To weave a new sly tale
As usual without fail
He's been on these big cakes
Things that he never bakes
And now he's boldly told
He's really not the gold
Just you follow the trend
And you can tell the end

11 June 2019

In Wrong Garments

She's been dancing
In our daughter's outfit
Since a long time ago

He's been strolling
In our son's apparel
Day after day

Are we both wrong?
Have we been moving about
In wrong garments?

11 June 2019

Private Jets

I want to fly in private jets
But I've now received many bets

Now I want those privately owned
I've seen myself already crowned

Your support is not just to pray
But willingly your levies pay

You need more blessings through prayers
You too prove you are good players

Our ministry cannot be last
So now redeem your pledges cast

12 June 2019

Not Impossible

It's not really that impossible
To stumble unto the possible
Not everything is plausible
But anything is proposable

12 June 2019

Bumpy, Yawning and Gory

There she lies long and winding
Like a ravenous desert snake
Opening out her chest
Full of bumpy scars and deep wounds
Momentarily hugging users
But mostly violently rocking
Often causing them to fumble and tumble
Crashing in their already dented vessels
See how she's forced
To suck generous blood
Spilled from dozens of mangled bodies

We've cried out ceaselessly
To the baobab trees
Near and far
For timely cure of
Her bumps and yawning wounds
Silence always, silence
Some of her ribs are already breaking
On her once-smooth chest
Only chest used for daily cruising
In variously dented vessels for
Various reasons to various
Destinations near and far
We sounded the early warning
To avoid the worst now already seen

Many seasons have come
And gone, silence still, eerie silence
Now the bumps on her chest
Are turning more rugged
The deep sores
Gaping and scary
And she's daily sucking up involuntarily

Blood of dozens of busy users
Making obituaries, dirges and eulogies
The permanent anthem
On our tired lips and drums

12 June 2019

The Extroverted Visitor

I like to be that outgoing, extroverted baby
Who's no stranger in any newly visited place
I like to behave just like that young proud lady
Who's comfortable at first visit to the palace
I like to be that bold African child who sees
London and NY as quarters of his basic village
Though I know I've crossed the seas
I'm from Africa doesn't grade me vintage

13 June 2019

Privileged Choice

I
Have an eye
On that pretty lad
Told the story to my dad
Since as palace lass I'll make
The privileged choice who I'll take
But after I did I was told palace can't
Take his kind into it which makes me pant

14 June 2019

Gives Me That Inner Fire

Call me Ekpe
Not that borrowed name
My senior brother, Linus, tagged on me
Before school admission and church baptism
Tagged that so I was not branded Biafra
A rebrand of the name Nigeria

Call me Ekpe
That's the name I truly cherish
The name that gives me that inner fire
That pride that every human enjoys
Not the one that destroys my identity
And lowers my dignity
Making me feel like a slave, tattooed
With a strange name
Robbing one of that human dignity
Ekpe is my name
Call me by it
I need that inner fire

Call me Ekpe
It is the name given me by my late father
I must honour and obey my father
Gone to join the ancestors
To intercede for me his only son
Left on planet earth
Inyang Awor Anyam Awor
Although being a staunch Catholic
Praying each day before he sees the sun
And before the moon takes control
People called him Anton
A Korup rebrand for Tony
As I later came to know it's short for Anthony

Call me Ekpe
My aunts, Ngwon and Oroka Awor
Hailed him, which taught me my lineage
Inyang Awor Anyam Awor of Beyatang
A powerful family in the village of Ekon
The cultural capital of Korup
An ethnic group with the small foot on Nigeria
And the big foot on Cameroon
The two nations once in bitter conflict
Over the oil-rich peninsular of Bakassi
Conflict that almost exploded into big flames
But luckily was stopped before the worst
Not only because a foreign body
Came in between but more so because
As same eggs are laid on both lands
Fiery anger couldn't let stones be thrown

14 June 2019

River of Blood

We all saw them on the wide screen
Leaning towards each other
In what to many of us appeared to be
A handshake, a sign of friendship
Which made the whole wide world
Read some hope for reconciliation
Between the two great ridges
Which for decades had stood
With such a steep valley between them

The encounter seemed to suggest
A possibility of building a bridge
To connect the two for real good
But it turned out to be something
Of obvious hypocritical content
And it soon became crystal-clear
The valley was instead developing
Into a new Qattara Depression
Or a much larger version of the Rift Valley
With absolutely no hope of a bridge

Suddenly lightning from the ridge
On the left flank tore the evening sky
And it was clear a great storm would soon
Rock the ridges as thunder cracked
Repeatedly without even rumbling
Which to most of us was so strange
Soon houses could be seen bowing
Swaying, roofs flying away, giving in to
The overwhelming storm and strangely
The valley was a river of pure blood
Bodies are seen sprawling on the land

Something inhabitants had never seen

14 June 2019

Youth of Africa

Youth of Africa
In village community
No voice
No meaningful place
In traditional council for decision-making

Youth of Africa
In local government
No role in town planning
No space for useful input in development

Youth of Africa
In national government
No strategic position
No meaningful role in politics and economy

Youth of Africa
Creative, inventive, innovative
No encouragement, no support
No recognition by village or government

Youth of Africa
Great talent, huge potential
Unleashed, untapped
To prosper village, nation and continent

Youth of Africa
Frustrated, angry, engaged in myriad vices
Easily swayed to join armed groups
Burn village, cripple nation, paint Africa poorly

Youth of Africa
Fleeing daily for safe havens
Rushing out for greener pastures

Feel neglected, see no clear future

Youth of Africa
Need initiatives for self-empowerment
Strong platforms to inspire productive sharing
Space for transformational leadership

15 June 2019

Mini Ma Okuma

A kwaka mung?
Se mi n turng

Chang mi andohn a kakpai
N ba re nongha rard na kakpai

Nik n sad nirn nimi
N ba chorn mini

Mbe reke mini ma okuma
A ya a o ru esin o re muki dotuma?

15 June 2019

Name the Founders

Dad trekked for days without bagging a rat
But he was really lucky to have founded Erat
He said his father discovered much kikon
In a rocky, hilly area which he named Ekon
Uncle, lost in a forest, struggled for anaku
Mushroom and named the place Ekonganaku

16 June 2019

Woman

Who carried man in the womb for
Good nine moons?
Woman.
Who birthed man?
Woman.
Who can bear the pain of childbirth?
Woman.
Who carried man until he was
Big enough to refuse being carried?
Woman.
Who breastfed and spoon-fed him?
Woman.
Who taught him how to
Crawl, stand, walk, run, and jump?
Woman.
Who first taught him how
To use language?
How to sing?
Woman.
How to dance?
Woman.
How to work?
Woman.
How to play?
Woman.
Even how to fight?
Woman.
Who has been doing more of
The care-taking until now?
Woman.
Who's been doing the carrying most of
The time even now that man is big?
Woman.
Who says woman is a weak?

Weak man.
Who says she's weak?
Weak man.

16 June 2019

How It Should Be

Let the breeze blow softy, softly
for trees
to nod their heads in same rhythm
and birds to fly about with ease
as flowers show their brightly-colored heads
sweet scents opening our blocked nostrils
That's how it should be

Let the clouds shift freely in the blue sky
let them keep turning, like folding mats
let them change their skin from white to black
and form generous rain
we badly need
That's how it should be

Let the rain pour gently from the sky
let it pour when it's its turn
like never before
after the soil has been badly scourged
leaving our river a parched earth
let it pour and feed our dying crops
That's how it should be

Let the rain feed our only river
emaciated river that can't even move
let it flow and regain its full currents
so the fish can freely swim
so we shall not die of thirst
nor lack seafood
That's how it should be

And when the sun takes sway again
let it shine and dry topsoil
subsoil left moist and fresh

let it not fry our river again
let it spare our mourning crops
only helps them make their food
That's how it should be

Let the seasons show some kindness
let them come and go in peace
leaving behind joy, abundance, hope
taking nothing belonging to us
making us always want to watch them
as they take freely their turns
That's how it should be

Let's create our vision anew
so our frightful dreams may soon regain
their childhood sweetness
smiles and laughter beaming wrinkled
faces in deep sleep, waking
greeted by sweet songs of songbirds
That's how it should be

16 July 2019

Soft Breeze

Feel the softness of the breeze
that rushes in
listen to the music
between the leaves
open your heart and let the music steal
steal away your worries and your fears
open widely and let it drop in
the sweet parcel it bears for you

16 June 2019

Strange Creatures

the hooting owl
with visage like your own
you quickly searched for words
and rebranded
witch-bird that brings you misfortune

the crawling snake
with shape like monkey's tail
if not like worm
that in your stomach dwells
you name serpent 'cos some do bite

these 'strange creatures'
that you treat with so much hate
may be the reason you've lost a trillion
rats with which you once shared house
that stole your food and ate your shoes and feet

16 June 2019

Kwona a Neryin Nebon

(Remembering the families of Korob)

I kpewi no
> neryin nebon

Ko i be re
> chirna no

Nik neryin ne boi
> ko ise ibon i rud

Nik ise ibon i monghene
> ko Korob ke karng

Besen
> be se no mung?

Besiwarn
> be warni bameng?

Buneu
> be newi mung?

Beyatang
> be tangha a ning?

Beyatoka
> be toka meng kwern?

Bokom
> be komi mung?

Batoanchok
> be choki mung ungo?

Kenei kebini
>be binene mung ndio?

Banunum
>be numi tor meng?

Buyern
>be chang mbohn neyern nawang?

Boku
>be yani kikuku

Bemad
>be chomi ukwern na emad

Bokumoto
>be chom moto mawang?

Backohk
>beh chomi dukoko da kohchohk

Bakoko
>be chom ikpo a deken da okoko

Borohna
>be chom ikpo a rohna ra uyin

Borukisangha
>be ya bisangha ba buperd

Bamang
>be kohmi mang neken na ichab?

Bamunerd
>be se kwern a meng kened?

Bokord
>be kohmi mang kord ka ekan?

Beyaborng
    be bornghi derng mung?

16 June 2019

We Fear and Hate Nature's Frown

We send out
Long-distance missiles
Across our shared sky
With shameless impunity

imagine
lightning cutting across
the sky incessantly for just a day

We send out battalions to menace
Armless men, women and children
In bullet-proofs, armored cars, warplanes
Without pity

imagine
a million elephants, giant eagles invading
each village, town and city for just a week

We bombard villages, towns and cities
With machine guns, grenades, bombs
In endless, heartless, senseless battles
Killing millions in cold-blood

imagine
thunder, storms, hurricanes
rocking our earth for just a month

We use war weapons
Without remorse, for years running
But can't stand the force of nature
Lightning. Thunder. Storms. Hurricanes

imagine
big cats, buffalos, elephants

in millions in our cities for just a year
Nature's frown we fear and hate to experience
Lightning, thunder, storms, hurricanes
Yet we burn and bomb, villages, towns
And cities in terrible show of force

17 June 2019

Nature of Nature

You fear to hear of acid rain
climate change, global warming
but fill the air with pollution

You don't wanna hear of species extinction
not even scarcity of plants and animals
but support logging, poaching and pollution

You hate to dream of earth without life
but keep destroying and polluting
plants, animals, that which is nature

Do you understand the nature of nature
the interconnectedness and interdependence
how it functions to support your life?

17 June 2019

Dog's Desire

I need life
out of the cage, without a chain
away from the cold
out from under the table
sitting on the chair
dining at the table

I need
a soft and gentle touch
on my forehead
a warm hand
caressing my cheeks
a big hug of human love and care

17 June 2019

Tell Your Story Yourself

Tell your story yourself
Don't let him narrate it to the world for you
He will give it twists you won't like
Tell your story yourself

Tell your story yourself
Don't let him choose the clothes you wear
To go out for that event
He will choose what will make you look different
And this will give you a new name
Tell your story yourself

Tell your story yourself
Don't let him do a haircut for you without your directives
He is not familiar with the tufts and contours of your hair
He will give you an ugly cut
That will give you a funny shape
Tell your story yourself

Tell your story yourself
You are big, have a good memory and power of orature and literature
Don't let him distort it for you
Tell your story yourself

17 June 2019

Share to Save The World

Don't be selfish

share every good thing in your head
share with others
share to save mankind

Those great skills you possess
show them at work to others
everything you've created
display for others to see and learn

You have good technologies
hide these not
transfer them to those in need
every new invention, share to save the world

17 June 2019

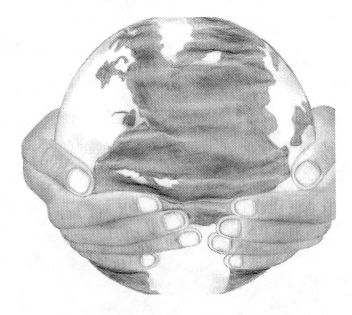

The Trick of Sleep

Sleep, so, so sweet; sweet, sweet sleep
squatting on my little eyelids.
It starts like under the influence of
a sleeping pill, a sleep potion,
or the feeling one gets on listening to a lullaby.

Soon my eyelids are heavy;
I can feel sleep really weighing in on my eyelids,
and my eyeballs have started rotating. Oh, sweet feeling!
Then, suddenly, I find myself
in this dense forest where my uncle, a hunter

used to take me for hunting.
Trekking barefoot behind my uncle
in the tropical moist forest is
training to become a man, a real man,
a tough man ready to face the rough world.

I often thought – indeed, always thought – sleeping
was time purely for relaxation, time to free
the mind of fear and stress. But here I am, working,
trekking behind my uncle after the hard day's
work, chatting, singing, dancing, and jumping with friends.

Suddenly, I jump aside. Ants are all over the place.
Why is it that my uncle often stops
where there are these terrible ants?
Is it another form of initiation into maturity, into manhood?
Another training on perseverance, on becoming a real man?

He has just seen some flash-eyes,
and has beckoned on me to stand still here,
right here where there are these irritating ants. But I can't,
no, I can't! I start to scatter the dead, dry leaves with my

tiny feet, making a hell of rattling noise in this dead of night.

And soon a distinct sound: the animal is happily running
away, safely away from my uncle's hot cartridge.
But my uncle is following swiftly, picking his way softly,
making sure his footsteps make no sound
to scare the animal all the more. But it's too late, too late.

My uncle keeps following. He's gone far afield. I can no longer
see the tongue of light from his fast-rusting carbide lamp
on his forehead. An uneasy silence - like a strange cloud -
is now closing in on me. Another test of maturity, staying
in this total darkness in a forest full of eerie

sounds of birds, insects, and some nameless weird creatures?
Snakes! No, no, no, don't even think of these! A young man once
bitten by a deadly type and killed in this adventure. Seems like
nocturnal life teems with frightful and lethal creatures.
Oh, now I can hear the sound of an owl, so close to where I stand.

It's becoming more than mere initiation into manhood - It's an ordeal!
My uncle's stayed so long, yet no sound of his gun, no gun sound
to reassure me of any human presence in this stretch of the world.
Is he still alive? Or is he lost in the maze of the tropical rainforest?
I'm already feeling nervous, now shivering uncontrollably.

Suddenly, in the far, far reaches where my eyes can carry me,
I can see, between numerous tree stems, twining lianas and thick foli-
age,
a faint flicker of hope, an unsteady light flashing intermittently.
But now it has vanished again, so abruptly; and my mind
is now taking me to frightful stories my old uncle, Obon Osere,

used to tell us in the heat of day, stories about a wild forest man
with a large nose the size of a huge Ekwe metal gong, Ekwe
the greatest society of Korob. Why is my mind taking me there?
To torture me in this chilling fear already swallowing me up
in this heart of the forest, in the oldest jungle of the world,

in this dead of night? I am forcing my mind to take me away, to one
of those jolly afternoon play scenes, one of those happy moments
playing with some funny friends; but it's still bringing me right back
to that story about the forest man, painted in "Ituror" song, that
fearsome man, in the deep of the forest, with such a huge nose and

wandering and searching eyes like those of an owl on a hunting mis-
sion.
I can hear the sound of the owl again - that same owl - frightening
me all the more. A deliberate act from this creature with face like hu-
man?
Such strange stories about owls, stories about their spiritual relation-
ship
with humans, as totems of some great witches and wizards of Korob,

past and present. My heart is pounding hard in this hot, confusing,
unprepared-for battle. Clear battle with some strange forces.
Battle with myself, battle with some witches, wizards and forest spirits.
Battle with everything uncanny you can imagine.
Then, suddenly, I see the light again, this time

reassuringly near enough; and my heart
is starting to beat less fast, and I give this joyful heave of relief.
Yes, I am now feeling some human presence.
Yes, my uncle is right here - around the corner - quite near
where I've been standing so helplessly like a statue for ages.

"Where are you", comes his unmistakable
voice as he clears his throat and spits
out a thick lump of phlegm as if to assure me he's the one.
I answer fearfully – nervously – in the certain belief that
he will give me another heavy conk on my forehead.

I'm starting to rehearse quickly how to absorb and manage
that excruciating pain from the callused knuckles of his smallish
left hand with missing thumb. His hunting badge, his only award.
He clears his throat again and shoots out another thick lump
of phlegm, which has only narrowly escaped landing

right on my little, round head. Suddenly, I find myself in my small
bamboo bed in my uncle's sooty thatched house, lying, soaked
in profuse sweat. I can't really explain what happened. Where's my
uncle?
Is life an inexplicable blend of consciousness and unconsciousness?
Reality and unreality? When did I arrive home and went
straight to bed without a clue? It's so, so real. The trick of sleep.

17 June 2019

There is Hope

When I come across
someone like you, someone
so beautifully made with illuminating decorum
I see a ray of hope dancing merrily on the horizon

there's still hope for a better world

When I come across
someone like him here that you've so richly favoured
someone so wonderfully kind, caring and loving
I feel we can easily calm the raging sea

there's still hope for a better world

I've met people like you not only here in this ailing land
but also in Sweden, Finland, India, Canada, Scotland,
Hong Kong, Sierra Leone, Nigeria, Kenya, Uganda...
even in America known for the craziest but most talented people on
earth

there's still hope for a better world

17 June 2019

Follow Me

Follow me,
follow the light I point
towards the darkest corners of the land,
follow me.

Follow me,
follow my voice and footsteps, follow me
out of the dark now swallowing you,
follow me.

Follow me,
follow the powerful musk of my skin, follow me
out of that dungeon called life,
follow me.

Follow me,
follow the path I create,
meandering, though, it may seem,
follow me.

Life is not a linear journey;
its path, therefore, cannot be straight.
Follow the winding path I create to avoid and to escape,
just follow me.

17 June 2019

Man of The Time

Julius in time hits the hot bottoms
Uncovering the truth about our land
Liberating us from centuries' plunder
Interpreting to us democratic principles
Unheard of from any of our kind
Since the days of great Mandela

Malema, indeed, is man of the time
Africa must use as an emblem of
Liberation, land restoration and equality
Enacted by that yearning for self-dignity
Made not to bow to manipulative forces
Always articulate, making strong points

20 June 2019

Act Like You?

To be your friend
I mustn't dress like you
Look like you
Think like you
Talk like you
Go where you go
Do what you do
And act like you

21 June 2019

It's Just a Bend

You're still on that journey
Been on it ever since
You gave your first cry and laugh
And took your first step
After your first cold bath
And now the road seems
To continue no more
You've hit the end, a weak voice says
But that great voice tells you strongly
Give you up not, carry on
It's just a bend

You are digging for water
Silver, gold and diamond
Digging for things to make the journey smooth
But suddenly you hit that hard rock
Hope seems completely lost again
Further tries clearly are wasted efforts
The weak voice says you can't go any deeper
But that strong voice again comes down
Courage, my son; faith, my daughter
Go on digging with even more hope
It's just a bend

You've been in this great battle so long
To calm the storm raging the land
You've searched your toolbox for
Great devices
Brought from those tall ivory towers
Applied this tool and that
Put in place this and that team of wits
Sent them out on missions on missions
It's been a moment of sweat and blood
But everything seems abortive

Yet that strong voice again remains so sure
It's just a bend

Now I see right in front of you
Water silver, gold, diamond aplenty
Great teams and tools right there ready
To shut down the battlefield
Dry your sweat and stop the bloodshed
Make the journey smoother
Than ever before imagined
You take a step and hit a toe on a rock
You take a second and hit it on a rod
A third you take but hit it no more
You hit that toe just at the bend

21 June 2019

To the Point of the Ridiculous

It can be as efficacious
As it can be malicious
To use words opprobrious
Enough to be so contagious
As to make the righteous
Appear so, so unrighteous
Receive threats contemptuous
From those not so courteous
But are always so cautious
Not to deal with the riotous
In atmosphere not so serious
But sometimes appears bilious
In the eyes of those injurious
To the point of the ridiculous

22 June 2019

The Sun Flower

At sunrise you show off your great beauty
Like carbide lamps of hunters on duty
Displayed exuberantly in forest in fine rows
In the distance croaky sounds of crows
Pouring in perpetual nature's celebration
In the village dance steps in perfect calibration
At sundown I hear this change in the tunes
Like hot deserts' rolling sand dunes
I lift my head to see those colours' brightness
Vanished, gone! All I now see is darkness
Turning happy celebrations into mourning
Phenomenon so far-fetched in the morning

22 June 2019

Nemesis

Nemesis
With teeth and fangs
And talons and claws
Crowned on Master Devil, the fire spirit

Nemesis
The spirit that spits fierce tongues of fire
On diggers of graves for the innocent
Nemesis
I see you moving around, nemesis

23 June 2019

Saying Sorry

You step on that dog's foot
After pouring cold, dirty water on her
Oh, hear how she screams
You just walked away
You can't say sorry

You told a lie against this person and that
After raining insults on them for no reason
You just walked away
You can't say sorry

You took a lady's handbag by mistake
After leaving yours behind that looks like hers
She rushes to you with your bag
You take yours from her and give her hers
And just walk away, as you can't say sorry

Saying sorry is not your habit
Saying sorry is sign of weakness
Saying sorry is something you can't do
Yes, you can't say sorry

23 June 2019

The Secret of Knowing

The secret of knowing
Is not to play the knowledge bank
No matter how much
Already absorbed
Displayed
Presented for expert weighing
Backed by emblems
Earned in the heat and sweat
In the race to attest

The secret of knowing
Is to note that which is in us so big
Is less than a grain in the sand
The brain's so copious to absorb
Far more than already stored
Let the mind be open
Eyes wide open
Ears pricked
Senses alert
Spirit, Body and Soul prepared
Ready to take in the bubbling, puzzling
Oceans of unknown knowledge
Wells of rare wisdom

The secret of knowing
Is to know there's much, much more
Loaded in cosmos, floating everywhere
Way away
About and around us
Under our noses
Waiting for that humble moment
Of thirst to learn

In full knowledge that
There's much, much more yet unknown

23 June 2019

The Journey

The journey had not been really smooth
Before my cradle it was hard like a tooth
Aton took Offiong across very swift rivers
To find out the truth about the drivers
Of the delay for the house to conceive
Not to trust those dreams that deceive
He had heard about that great seer
Whose home was near that of the deer
Across rivers that had claimed lives
Across forests with teeming bee hives
Aton and Offiong braved all these for me
To bring me forth so I can like others be
Part of those this stretch will forge to grow
So all and sundry live to dance and crow

24 June 2019

That Picture

That picture is still firm and sharp
Stamped on my memory wall
Picture picked at childhood
When uniformed men visited
Villages, asking for tax receipts
My uncle who also apparently
Had nothing at all to show
Was dragged out of his abode
Given several blows on the head
With a club the size of a mortar pestle
I can see the liquid dripping steadily like
Divided rivers down his face in bright red
Couldn't associate it with invitation
To the world beyond, poor me
Today I see a repainting of
That picture in crueler ways

26 June 2019

The Beauty of Living

The
beauty of living
resides
in the cheerful home of loving;
The
beauty of loving
dwells
in the joyful heart of sharing;
The
beauty of sharing
lies silently
in the simple hands of humility.

28 June 2019

Genuine Power

Ngwa, never let bilious anger
Gain a better part of you.
Win love, as usual, by giving more love
And, in return, you'll receive, believe me,

Bridget, the biggest share of joy and happiness
Residing deep inside you,
In your heart of endless care.
Destroy every iota of hate, and
Gain a well of love and peace
Each and every time you
Treat others with genuine love.

Ngum means power, mighty power,
Genuine power of love for a lasting
Union with God, the only
Mighty One we on earth gladly share.

30 September 2019

Like the Soil

(Inspired by Radhanath Swami's analogy of Bee and Fly)

Be like the searching bee
Bypassing
The rubbish mountains in you
And landing on
The flower deserts you have
In search of nectar,

Not like the hunting fly
Bypassing
The flower paradises in you
And landing on
The rubbish deserts you have
To feast on rotting particles;

Be like the silent soil
On whom every
Rubbish species we daily dump
But who, in return,
Blesses us with abundant crop,
Averting impending famine.

30 June 2019

One Africa

Let's bring up
The rich nutrients of history
Dig into the mine wells of
Long lost memory
And see the picture clearly of
One Africa

Let's work on
The pieces of broken bricks
Broken by political divide
Fragmentation that tears us apart
And see the picture that once was of
One Africa

Let's work on
The broken artifacts, fitting the puzzles of
Art, culture, commerce and governance
Science, technology and economy
And see how really powerful we were as
One Africa

Let's work on
The fragments of civilization
Go back to the very cradle, and
Reflect on what went wrong, why it all died
And fuel that spirit in kids and teenagers today
Who give a new chorus of the greatness of
One Africa

Let's work on
The ingenuity expressed
Daily by those kids and teenagers
Building bulldozers, trucks, cars, planes
Adults looking on with unseeing eyes

Thinking it's yet children at play in that
One Africa

1 July 2019

Life is a Poem

i.
Life is a poem
Written
By
The invisible, only living
Ancient Poet
As sweet sonnet
On fine sheets of sand
From primordial
Time and space
Millennia
Before
It is lived on this ball of dust

ii.
Life is a poem
Written
In words
So
Esoteric
And
Shrouded in
Clouds of
Dazzling black, brown, and white
In language
Unintelligible
To mortal beings

iii.
Life is a poem
Written
In letters
Not
In the least

Legible
And thus
Incomprehensible
By mortals
Yet read
With such flair and ease
By spirit beings

iv.
Life is a poem
Written
To
Twist
And twirl, puzzle, and blow
The mind
And lift
And lower the spirit
And to finally transport
The soul amidst celestial music
To confound and leave
The mortals in mourning gowns of cloud

v.
Life is a poem
Bearing
The body
In fine sheets of silk
Swinging and lulling it in earthly space
While drifting
The mind
Slowly
But surely Into
That magnificent fogginess
That heavenly space, just a bend away
Where angels hover in wait

vi.
Life is a poem
Written with

A mystery pen
On
Blank sheets of sand
In vapourising
Ink
Like colours
Of the rainbow
Vanishing
Kaleidoscopically
Miraculously into heavenly void

vii.
Life is a poem
Interpretable by
None
But the Bard
Himself
On the last day, in great ceremony
When angels shall
Read
Each poem line by line
Against the rhythm of life
Lived
On this putrid ball of dust

2 July 2019

Fighting for Titles

I watch them almost daily
Scurrying to climb to the top
Using crooked ladders of con
Stabbing others in the back
Drawing attention from bosses
Fighting for greater titles
For power to also be in charge

7 July 2019

Reading the Stars

The moon is in its full form
Sits she in the dark starry sky
I look up and see the stars
Forming letters that a story tell
A great story it must be
A story that points the way
The easy way to everything
But I'm so illiterate in the signs
And need someone greater
Wise enough read the stars for me

7 July 2019

Amened

My prayers I've oft amened
By God they have been amened
My predicaments amened

7 July 2019

An Ode to Mani Offiong

The cockcrow woke me to a new dawn
And I saw this new great picture drawn
It was a picture of Mani Offiong drawn

And I thought of that time when she carried
Me in her warm arms when I tarried
Yes, when my wearied legs surely tarried

It was a long trek from Erat back to Ekon
Then no music to listen to of Akon
No, no star then with the name of Akon

Erat was so, so, so far away
Trekking made the child's mind sway
Yes, my childhood memory did sway

When shall the journey reach the end?
Each time we came to a new bend
Always there was a new bend

Soon I could hear the crow of cock
Like ship I could feel the near of dock
And I thought no distance to the dock

Another hour might have ticked past
Yet the ship had not shown its mast
Ekon still a distance from our mast

I could hear a cock's assuring crow still
Yet more bends and now another steep hill
Mani carried me in her arms on that hill

Bag on back, she pointed to a thatched house
Soaked in sweat was her travel blouse

Nice we're home for her to dry her blouse

That's what had been her long story
In soaked blouse as she rode the lorry
Of her life, story carried by the lorry

Mani was among life's great eleven players
Who knelt each morning for prayers
And, indeed, answered were her prayers

7 July 2019

The Elephant

Have you ever seen the elephant live?
I know you've seen it more in pictures,
Moving and still; so interesting, isn't it?
Charismatic, keystone, flagship species!
Seen the trunk? Very like a big snake!
Indeed, a prehensile hand!
And the ears? Like huge ceiling fan blades!
Seen it's tail to whisk off tse-tse flies?
And huge tusks attractive to poachers?

There exist two types of elephant -
Savannah elephant, forest elephant,
The savannah type a little bigger.
Elephant, elephant, elephant, elephant,
Biggest terrestrial animals in size
But not in population ever dwindling
Due to poaching and habitat shrinkage
From rising deforestation more for timber
But also for roads and huge plantations
Driving herds to farms and plantations,
Bringing these in conflict with us
As they display their crop-raiding behaviour.

Know anything good about the elephant?
Research findings by Dr. James Powell
And other top researchers on the mammal:
Seeds of more than fifty species of plant
Germinate only after passing through
It's guts that serve as treatment chambers
In the laboratory of life and sustainability.
That it forages on such a wide variety
And in such great bulk also means
It's huge guts-wastes surely enrich
The thin forest soils and serve as mediums

For species to disperse and sprout to life
In areas that never once saw them,
The elephant enjoys such a huge home range.
It's behaviour of pushing down trees
Opens up the canopy for sunlight to hit
The forest floor, giving life to dormant seeds,
Causing shade-suppressed species
To pick up and swim towards their fullness,
Ensuring the very health of our forests
That consume tons of carbon dioxide
To stabilize our climate changing.

9 July 2019

Home First

He spends his time
Never giving a dime
Of attention to rhyme
He loves not crime
But things so prime
His love for home
So strong like bone

10 July 2019

Five Lessons from Mom Son

(In memory of my mother)

Deny not anyone food
if just a little more
than you need to stay alive;
An escort you won't be
of anyone to toilet to undo.

Go out not with a woman
beautiful, elegant but married;
Better go for that ugly
And free lady, and be forever free.

Laugh not at and insult not
the poor nor those
with any form of infirmity;
Only after death will
your own complete story
on earth be known.

Refuse not the old
a pinch of snuff begged for;
A rare moment that might be
to sit and listen to advice
your life for good change.

Hesitate not to harken
to a sudden call from the old;
A critical moment that might be
your life in danger to rescue.

11 July 2019

A Philosophical Joke

Every human has
three pairs of eyes

Those to observe
the form and state of body

Those to decipher
the state of heart and mind

Those to discern
the state of spirit and soul

11 July 2019

Writing Poetry

Writing poetry
Heals me;
Neatly puts
The broken pieces
Of my psyche
Together;
Refreshes my brain,
Nourishes my soul,
Multiplies my capacity
A hundredfold,
Making me feel
Like a genius
That I never thought
I could become.

11 July 2019

Awor Anya

Awor Anya
Orom a one

Awor Anya
Charb a nenen

Awor Anya
Obon a uyin

Awor Anya
One a kebern

Erekwa a biri
Kpang dotoko

Erekwa a biri
Men munok

Erekwa a biri
Chorn mini

A eno a
A Awor Anya

A ka sou a eno a meng
U ba ewerb?

Awor Anya
I ka wohng ngo

Awor Anya
I ri chirna ngo

Awor Anya

Abama o! Abama o! Abama o!

Awor Anya
Nik Obasi o nami kohm

Kankanghana
Kengo a duchorn!

12 July 2019

Legacy

Work hard to leave behind
A legacy
A legacy not of havoc to society
But of positive impact on society
Impact on individuals around you
Impact on your community
Impact on your nation and continent
Impact on the world
And let your conscience be your only
Assessment tool
In determining whether
And at which level you have
Left behind the legacy

12 July 2019

Not All Men

Many men
Are
Made to be crafty
Clever, tricky, cunning
Thieving

Not all men
Are
Made to be human
Gentle, caring, loving
Selfless

Not all men
Are
Made to be wise
Thoughtful, insightful
Fair, just, prudent

Not all men
Are
Made to be deathless
Leaving behind
A legacy
Bold footprints
On the sands of time

12 July 2019

Your Turn

It is your turn
To restart
- Not to start -
What you started
A long time ago
But surely allowed
To lie so dormant
Neglected that
It was stolen away
And refined
Using your resources
And sold back
To you like foreign
Knowledge
And products of
Sophistication
That now drain you
Dry and awe you
As you consume
With relish
That which now
Consume you
That which should
Should have been
Supplied by you
As original producer
Who now negotiate
The place of
Mere apprenticeship
Despite evidences of
Being the workshop master
The one bestowed
With the great ideas
The swelling knowledge

Skills and resources
To produce
The astounding products
For the rest of the world
By the simple
Evidence that
As you read this
Tiny little poem
Your smallest
Least expected of
Children from
Least expected of
Communities
Now produce
That which makes
Adults in faraway land
Look on with awe
But yet seem
To escape
Your authentic
Eyes and heart
To promote
And bring to the fore
And be also
Produced
For mass supply
In packages of
Flashy sophistication
To the rest of the world

14 July 2019

Under the Eyes of Deep Blue Sky

Sun had surely drifted
Gone to bed and seemed
To be snoring in deep, deep sleep.
Lying it seemed just above
The roof of my modest second
House I got in a few months as a new
Internally Displaced Person
In the coastal town following
The turmoil that hit Mount Fako.
Mount Fako sat there satiating beside
The seemingly snoring Sun that now
Casts a golden splash that melts
Lovingly into Atlantic in apparent
Readiness for a conjugal embrace.
Right from my balcony I could
See the deep blue sky playing
The Umpire as Mount Fako is
In obvious furious communication
With Atlantic that is already
Arranging a huge set of pillows
On a well-dressed bed ready for
The long-awaited moment
As Sun twists and turns
In romantic embrace of him.

18 July 2019

Great African Songs

Take this.
Hot and tasty.
Fresh from the fireside.
The source of
My creative imagination.
See the way
I do it with ease.
See the way
I make it flow
Like Blue Nile
Winding down to meet
Mediterranean.
Like Niger
Rushing to embrace Atlantic.
Like Congo
Pouring libation to the vast green.
Like Sanaga
And Orange and Limpopo
And Zambezi strolling down
Mandela Street in Soweto,
Hands interlocked with those of Winnie
In a terrific bond of comradeship,
Singing great African melodies
In Swahili, Zulu, in Durob, in Hausa.
Songs of hope, liberation, unity, peace.
Songs that could transform
The Sahara into a vast green.
In Swahili, songs of hope.
In Zulu, songs of liberation.
In Durob, songs of unity.
In Hausa, songs of peace.

19 July 2019

After that Period

After that moment's serious strain
And obvious total psychic drain
Give me your arms' warm shower
To regain some refueling power
After that period of hateful test
I certainly, really need some rest
To become completely refreshed
So I can feel I've been re-fleshed

22 July 2019

You Alone Must Enjoy

Just because I have it makes you
Eat up your heart since you don't
And you look for every means to
Level accusations on my poor self
Organising your friends to vent their
Utmost show of anger and disgust on me
Since only you and you alone must be up
You alone must all opportunities enjoy

24 July 2019

Morals Lost

(i)
We pray,
Children
Come;
Joy floods our homes.
Our role
We know so well -
Raising the children
In the best way.
A natural role,
Pure.
And
To give
The best possible
We strive.
Our best
Always we do
The best to give,
The very best.
Lessons of life we dish out
Daily.
In homes,
In churches,
In schools,
Preaching, singing:
Respect for others,
Especially for the elderly;
Grow in morality,
Display always
Behaviour proper and sound.
In the children
We do really cultivate
Love and care,
Society to make safe,

Peaceful, prosperous
Worthy of living.

(ii)
But see what,
Today,
Flank our streets,
Dress our holiday resorts.
Nudity displayed:
Modern dressing code
Held up like flag;
Statues at strategic places
Mounted to sell nudity
In all ramifications;
Stark nudity
Shamelessly, publicly
Displayed in our museums,
Near - no, not just near -
In shopping malls,
At city centres,
Everywhere.
In music,
In sundry selling work of art
Shown
Daily
On Television,
On Social Media; it's
Now such a drowning craze.
Acts of immorality,
Everywhere;
Acts of violence,
Everywhere, every minute.
Our children consuming these
With relish,
Their eyes and ears of ignorance
Feasting
In utter voraciousness.
Poor children
Deep in pools of

Sublime insanity
Helplessly swimming and bathing
Happily
In killing immorality
Displayed in bold ignorance
Everywhere
Under the clear, blue sky.

(iii)
Children,
Our children,
The world's children,
Children
We cared for so much
No longer carrying
The values expected,
No longer
Those we knew,
Those
We
Spent
Our life's treasures and energies
To raise;
They've now
Been wantonly destroyed,
Systematically
Consumed by shadows of
The dark past;
Primitive codes and acts
Now
Replayed,
Displayed
As great petals of
Civilization.
Society's clearly
Maddened by
Queer sparks of modernity.
Branding
Morality primitive now the norm;

Crusaders of morality
Regarded as
Living in the past;
The very past scenes of nudity
Hitherto termed primitive
Now hailed
And rewarded.
Moving nude in streets
Now
Branded modernity.
Civilization's
Truly turned
Inside out,
Upside down;
Immorality now considered
The perfect way of life.

27 July 2019

My New Ask from God

Lord
God I
Sincerely ask of
You to create new
Humans with wings to fly

Lord
Let them
Fly across territorial
Boundaries without being stopped
For undue checks by anyone

Oh
Lord God
Laws against moving
Across boundaries be abrogated
So we can move about

31 July 2019

Again

Again the man came, not
For gain but to rebuild
The broken bridges, and repair
Just across the ridges clear
In my country so, so dear

1 July 2019

Pendulum

The
Swinging from
Wing to wing,
Ticking to effect time.
Now I ask this simple
Question: In which wing is Pendulum?

Pendulum
Hitting this
Wing and that
Makes me think it
Is wingless, and has no
Defined place to come to rest.

The
Ticking so
Consistent, but swinging
Quite confusing. I can't
Tell whether or not Pendulum
Is in ours or in theirs.

Surely
The question
Can be answered
Only when Pendulum stops
To swing, to truly tell
The wing that keeps its seat.

1 August 2019

Turning Around

I've for long been showing you
Brotherly love, quietly observing
You put up those fake smiles;

But turning around,
Turning around,
And turning around;

Yes, as I turned around
To see your back I now know
What you've hidden from me.

Turning around,
Turning around,
And turning around

I now get what you've been
Saying in sly insinuations
Confirmed in great detail.

Turning around,
Turning around,
And turning around

I've seen the tortoise in you;
I've seen the python in you;
I've seen the scorpion in you.

1 August 2019

Truly

I've been listening keenly
To words you use
Daily
In conversation with me -
Written,
Verbal -
And I've been reading clearly
Your body language each time;
No message can be clearer.

But
You surely think I'm blind
To your intrigues,
Your
Evil plans towards me.
You wished I stood beneath,
Stooping low
To see you
Stand tall like the Iroko
You're aspiring to become,
Despite the obvious void in you.

Yes, yes, yes, a lot to learn. What a life!
But,
Like I've always said,
"A million demons
Can't stand the strength of
The one and only God -
Omnipotent, Omnipresent, Omniscient -
The God whom I serve
And trust."

Truly,
"What goes round

Comes round."
You see?
That hot arrow you've sent
Round to strike me and others you hate,
You now receive
In its total hotness and bitterness;
And you run
To me,
Your head on my shoulder to lean,
Still with your teeth
Buried deep in my flesh,
Biting so hard
But smiling so broadly -
A sly smile even a baby can tell -
And you think I'll think it's love?

Truly,
Being a staunch evildoer, you know not
Those you hurt feel, sense and see;
And you keep on playing
The evil game
Until the game now turns its wheels
Right round,
And
Starts
Playing itself
'Gainst you, while the innocent me
Stand looking on in awe,
Wondering
Why the reverse
In
Just a bend.

2 August 2019

Soprano

I heard the voice
In that special song
Dedicated to the Creator
A clear soprano
Sharp like razor
Smooth like a looking glass

Looked up to see the source
Saw this lady
Quite dressed in bulk
Met her to verify
And she shot it out to me
A soprano. Rare in quality. Unique

En route from Yaounde to Douala, 3 August 2019

Where Is the Love?

You go behind really stabbing me
Yet for you I've continued to be
You hurt me daily like a sly dove
And I ask, "Where is the love?"

You bathe me with praises clearly fake
What should be mine you surely rake
All my friends away you madly drove
And I ask, "Where is the love?"

Now I read your heartbeat of hate
That it's only now I read it is not late
I can my hand still rid of that glove
As I now ask, "Where is the love?"

You've been chopping at my roots
After they stole away my boots
You do this thinking not of He above
And I still ask, "Where is the love?"

Now it's your time to get your pay
You surely will not survive the day
Me you bit and now must surely rove
And I still ask, "Where is the love?"

5 August 2019

Filled with Lies

He fills his stomach with fried lies
Which he eats from dishes of gossips
Added to what he himself learnt to brew
In his pot of bitter, spiteful vengefulness
He suffers from serious stomach upset
And throws these up in public places
The obvious rubbish he's long stored
Receiving accolades instead of boos
And he continues throwing these up
The way journalists broadcast news
But one's raising a finger though
They all know these are hateful lies
Bombshells for those who challenge
Or try to prove they're also so tough

5 August 2019

Fill the Earth with Laughter

Fill the Earth with laughter
Rake out all brute liars
Dismiss all crocodiles
Push away tortoises
Impose more honesty
Bless creation with love
Build a world of real peace

5 August 2019

Reading Unintended Meanings

You read unintended meanings
Out of stories as simple and clear
And feel so hurt by what you read
Then you surely carry a load of guilt

5 August 2019

Poetry Tree

I've found a very wild tree
That bears great poems
Quite tall though it is
You must learn to climb

I tried to climb the tree
And I rolled right down
And I tried again to climb
And my eyes went aglow

And I looked right up
And I saw the great poems
Like fruits above my head
Hanging from huge boughs

And I reached out for one
And for more and more
Prof tasted these fruits
And he said all were good

5 August 2019

My Father's Singlet

When I look at that picture
Showing me in my three or so
In my father's singlet
The story comes right back
Afresh
Dad had bought me a black suit
Mom had dressed me
In that suit
Ready to take that
Family picture
My younger brother
(May his soul Rest In Peace)
Mom had dressed in Pinafore
Bright colour
And I cried out loud
I didn't like to be dressed in black
To take the family picture
I can't really explain why I didn't
And insisted on putting on
Something purely white
My father's singlet

5 August 2019

Time to Take a Break

Time to take a break
from
aimless search.
Time to reflect
on life lived.
On life
being lived.
On life
that should be lived.
Not
convoluted
nor brutally shattered;
not
crushed,
not
burnt,
not
wasted.

Time to take a break
from
aimless search.
Time to regain that lost moment
when the moon and stars
reflected wholeness
into my life.
When the one that was mine
was
my sweet breath.
Breath that pumped peace
into the ocean
of
my soul.
Breath that ceased before my eyes

on that cruel night
at a time
I needed it the most.
Genuine, sweet breath that used to be
my priceless cup of peace.
Breath blown away so soon,
so slowly,
ticking away
before my eyes,
and,
finally,
snatched
by that cruel, frigid night.

Time to take a break
from
aimless search.
Time to reflect
on
that night that emptied my dreams
through the porous funnel
and
into the frozen abyss of nothingness.
The dreams, I could sense,
tumbling down
the cliff of dilemma,
into the far recesses of void
and meaninglessness.
Tumbling down and
breaking the cord of peace
that once was
the permanent cutlery
on my table of life,
for my daily
breakfast,
lunch,
and sumptuous dinner.
Leaving me to dine,
henceforth, with bare,

quivering hands of stress
and helplessness.
Pushing me into fake, hot corners
devoid of care
and peace.
Peace that once was
pumped freely - generously -
into all channels of my soul...
in just a single
breath of pure love.
Love, love, love,
mother of peace.
Sweet mother that now I really
and
badly need
like never before.
To birth me more vessels of peace.

Time to take a break
from
aimless search.
A complete
breakaway from ways and things
of this cracking ball of dust.
A peaceful moment of
deep reflection I surely need.
A moment of redefinition, of
healing
of my scathed life.
A moment
to pick up new energy, new strength.
A moment of rejuvenation
after
that epoch of debilitation.
A moment to regain
that huge loss back into consciousness.
Recollections
and distillations into palpable realities
the priceless juice of love.

A moment to seal
the deep hole
in my frail heart.
A moment of certainty, of
renewed hope
for the best.
A moment of prayers
for the utmost best.
The very best ever hoped for.
Nothing
but the best.
The very, very best, the
soul-soothing
peace,
in
that huge gold cup,
brewed
by real, genuine love.
And surely
from that cup shall I drink
that peace again
soon.

6 July 2019

ABOUT THE AUTHOR

The 2014 winner of the Eko Prize for Emerging Anglophone Writers in the poetry category, **Ekpe Inyang** holds an MSc in Advanced Professional Studies (Environmental Studies) from the University of Strathclyde, UK. He spent several years working for the World Wide Fund for Nature (WWF) and Wildlife Conservation Society (WCS), and also served as a short-term consultant to the German Technical Agency (GTZ, now GIZ) in the South West Region, Cameroon. He was a lecturer and Coordinator of the Diploma in Development Studies Programme at the Pan-African Institute for Development – West Africa, in Buea, Cameroon, and currently the Capacity Building Advisor of WWF Coastal Forests Programme (WWF-CFP) and Education for Sustainable Development and Youth Focal Point for WWF Cameroon Country Programme Office (WWF-CCPO). He has published eight plays, four scientific articles, a book chapter, two major textbooks (one as co-author), and eight poetry anthologies, six of which have been published.

About Spears Books

Spears Books is an independent publisher dedicated to providing innovative publication strategies with emphasis on African/Africana stories and perspectives. As a platform for alternative voices, we prioritize the accessibility and affordability of our titles in order to ensure that relevant and often marginal voices are represented at the global marketplace of ideas. Our titles – poetry, fiction, narrative nonfiction, memoirs, reference, travel writing, African languages, and young people's literature – aim to bring African worldviews closer to diverse readers. Our titles are distributed in paperback and electronic formats globally by African Books Collective.

Visit us at www.spearsmedia.com

Connect with Us

Visit our Website
Go to www.spearsmedia.com to learn about exclusive previews and read excerpts of new books, find detailed information on our titles, authors, subject area books, and special discounts.

Subscribe to our Free Newsletter
Be amongst the first to hear about our newest publications, special discount offers, news about bestsellers, author interviews, coupons and more! Subscribe to our newsletter by visiting www.spearsmedia.com

Quantity Discounts
Spears Books are available at quantity discounts for orders of ten or more copies. Contact African Books Collectives at orders@africanbookscollective.com or Spears Books at orders@spearsmedia.com.

Host a Reading Group
Learn more about how to host a reading group on our website at www.spearsmedia.com

Printed in the United States
By Bookmasters